# Ifika Youika

## The journey through the eye of a songster

GW00702135

**Martin Hansard**

**Zodi Books**

Published by Zodi Books 2017

A catalogue record for this book is available from the British Library.

ISBN  978-0-9955767-0-4

Printed and bound in Ireland by Sprint Print

Zodi Books

zodibooks@hotmail.com

# Table of Contents

# Part One

# Pseudo-Punk

Night Fear

North Wall

Stone Age Blues

The Diamond

Saved

Persona non Grata

Busker

Music Business

Jay Walking

Mad Hatter

Beggars and Vagrants

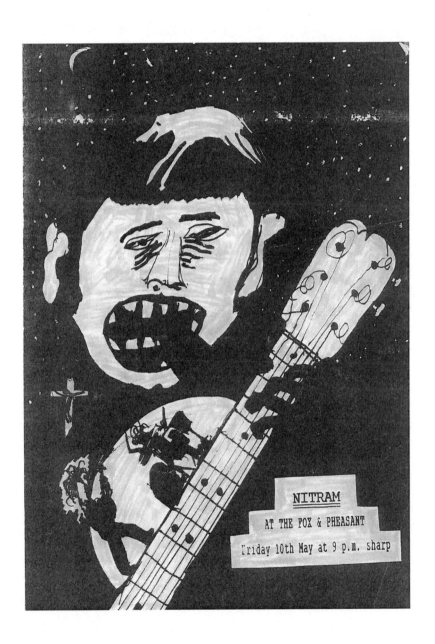

The boy was only three years old when he was given his first job; to put a silver shilling in the gas meter. The sound of the coin falling and spinning in the empty chamber coincided with the sound of music: a song. He followed the melodious calling back to the kitchen.

Who were the singing men who possessed such magic! Under the full force of their spell he lived in a dream world. Years later while reading the poets in English class his dream world re-awakened.

## Night Fear

Ooh the owl cried, ooh the owl dived
On the unwary rat that lived by its side
Silent the night broke by the cry of the owl
And silent the life went from Ratty Tra Trowl

Ratty Tra Trowl forgotten next day
His family were happy the owl flew away
No more they had sorrow no more they had grief
As the cold of the winter came leaf by leaf

But then one day the bad owl was seen
And the rats fled ever so keen
The owl dived again without one more sound
But the rats were not there so it fell to the ground

That sad night passed so early next morn
The body was found bruised up and torn
The owl said he feared the night not the day
And just at those words the owl passed away

The side streets and laneways between Ballybough Road and North Strand Road was the perfect place for a pubescent pseudo-punk rock a cappella street band to form. On the scrap of grassy no-man's land behind the Old Folks where the sodium hue of the distant street lights shone weakest, the Wild Zygotes practised their set: Outside the rundown shop on Clonmore Road all their friends were waiting to hear their latest number one.

## North Wall

I met Imelda Ryan down the docks
I said to her will you open your box
I said to her will you take a call
She said to me go down to North Wall, North Wall.....

I went down into town and met a girl in there
She was tall, trim, dark and slim and she had curly hair
I took her down to North Wall
But then she got the picture
When she knew what I was going to do
Then I really ditched her, North Wall, North Wall.....

I fell in love with a tramp last night
We kept on doing it 'til we got it right
Nothing happened between me and her
It was just the name of the street that's all
North Wall, North Wall.....

'Was your mammy a monkey was your daddy a baboon goon', he asked in all seriousness, trying to debunk the theory of evolution; intimating by his rhetoric that animals simply can't jump the species barrier and that humans didn't evolve from the ape and diversification was God's will.

His class of inner city adolescences reacted like apes jumping on desks and partaking in internecine group battles, revelling in the anarchy: 'Father Harry for Pope', they bellowed at the old priest.

## Stone Age Blues

You may evolve into a man
Into a homo sapien
But will you ever change
You may evolve another stage
Into a super-human sage
But will you ever change

Neanderthal man tell me about your stone age blues
Neanderthal man tell me about your stone age blues
Was your mammy a monkey
Was your daddy a baboon goon
Neanderthal man tell me about the dinosaur
Neanderthal man tell about thc dinosaur
Was Tyrannosaurus Rex really in your folklore

Neanderthal man tell about your politics
Neanderthal man tell about your politics
Did you make many laws
Were you really such a hypocrite
Neanderthal man tell me about society
Neanderthal man tell me about society
Were your children all junkies screaming for democracy

Neanderthal man tell me about the wars you waged
Neanderthal man tell me about the wars you waged
Was it really necessary to cause so much death and rage
Neanderthal man tell me about the clothes you wore
Neanderthal man tell me about the clothes you wore
Were you standing free and naked
Like a long, long time before

Neanderthal man tell me about polygamy
Neanderthal man tell me about polygamy
Did you slay all your brothers, keep your women at your knee
Neanderthal man tell me about theosophy
Neanderthal man tell me about theosophy
Were you frightened of the thunder
Or the vastness of the sea

The Gloucester Diamond was at the heart of the community, where the men gambled Toss the Coin, and the young played Piggy, Five-a-Side and Relieveo - it's winning refrain, 'all in, all in, the game is broke up' echoing in the tenement halls of Seán McDermott Street and Gloucester Place.

Large families were the norm: sixteen children in a two room flat with shared toilet, off landing.  There was a certain pride in saying 'I have eleven sisters and four brothers', and a certain mischievousness knowing what the reaction would be like. On their forty fifth wedding anniversary, their sixteen children pooled in and gave them a big party in the North Star Hotel.

## The Diamond

Something good went down a long time ago
When a pretty young girl met a working man
His name was Gally her name was Ellen
This is that story and I'm going to tell it

In nineteen forty-two they bought little shoes
For young Jimmy and Mary too
The Diamond was such a different place then
There was no need to lock your gate

You know how much you mean to me
You gave me eyes to see
The falseness of this world
And the strength to carry on

By the time John F. Kennedy was blown away
There were fifteen of us with Breda on the way
When the nights got cold you built a fire
To keep us warm to raise us higher

Without a cry, without a moan,
You kept us dry you kept us warm
Mother you loved us with all you had
Father you loved us, that wasn't bad

Anyone would have done the same, anyone. Anyone would have stepped down into the November chilled canal, even if the infant child was dead, a very human thing to do. Anyone would have pressed on its little chest if they saw the tiny stream of bubbles seeping from its pale blue lips. Anyone: but it happened to be you.

## Saved

Out on the waves we must go again
Into the storm as the night descends
Hold onto the rails tighter my friends
Look out for the flares and the drowning men
And there's always a time to be brave
And there's always a life to be saved

The call has come in of a boat in distress
Call out all the crew although they're bereft
Last time they came back there was five of them left
Seven went out and two met their death
And there's always a time to be brave
And there's always a life to be saved

The waves rise so high like a mountain of green
The boat is upturned but the sailors are seen
Floating away like seeds in a stream
Steady the bow and turn on the beam
And there's always a time to be brave
And there's always a life to be saved

The sea is too high, they're not able to swim
Throw the life-line we'll take them all in
A cargo of men and then we'll return
Back to the pier and all the loved ones
And there's always a time to be brave
And there's always a life to be saved

Blowing their wages at the bar, the apprentices were drunk with confidence, camaraderie and carefree independence. It was a Dead Poets Society for the working class, where poetry, music, literature and political science were passionately discussed in the influential company of the qualified men. Their very own Socrates; a senior electrician who had ten years on them, explained that some leading politician had become a 'persona non grata' because he was ostracised by his peers for serious political and personal indiscretions.

## Persona non Grata

A long time ago in the valley of pain
There lived a young man, said he'd come back again
And his name was Daddy to you

He spent some time in the government bin
He never knew nothing but pain and sin
And his game was nothing to lose

He sank right down to the lowest depths
That most men haven't experienced
And that's why he is King of the blues

One dark night he was young and mean
He doesn't want to relive that scene
But could lead you if you choose

The land he's from is a shabby place
Where people lie into your face
And if you're from there you're going to know

Where everybody is your friend
Until you find they just pretend
And Mister you'd better go

The only way to get along
Is to crush someone if they're not strong
Because if you don't Man, they do it to you

Where double think and double take
Go hand in hand with power, don't blink
And Sister you never knew

We seem to lose all of the love we crave
We stand accused but I know we can be saved

In Butter Lane and Grafton Arcade and under London's Marble Arch you play; in dark reverb. On Shop Street on a March morning, blowing steamy breath on numbing finger tops and stamping hard to feel your toes. Projecting your life force, singing at the world, soul naked: constructing a new you from scratch. Connecting so fleetingly to the passerby who stops mid stride; returns; a glance of coy appreciation, aims weighty coins into your hat, then walks back to her normal day.

## Busker

There's a place and a time
In everyone's mind
And everyone wants to feel free
If you throw me a coin
I'll promise next time
I won't be so hard on your dreams

There's this man in my brain
Trying to explain
Time is a thing that won't yield
There's a girl with a book
Trying not to look
Each time that I can't reach the key

The radio bleats
The news of the week
I wish you could get in my head
Because I know you would find
A place and a time
Where everything's kept warm and fed

There's no war on the streets
Everything's cheap
And pain is a word that's not said
And the children rule
From a class in their school
The old folks can all rest in bed

I want to sing like a child
Free and unspoiled
So unaware of conceit
If you throw me a coin
I'll promise next time
I'll make you stand up on your feet

The streets of youth are awash with the coalition of the willing: willing to give at their own expense, their time and talent to promoters and profiteers in the vague hope of making the grade. And in the business of war, when weapons of mass destruction reach their sell by date and new technologies need testing, new theatres always open up.

## Music Business

I hate the music business, Man
The one where you have to pay to play
I hate the music business, Man
This songwriter is nothing but a slave
I just thought I'd learn to play guitar
I just thought I'd write another bar for you

My hopes of fame faded fast
No A&R man wants to lick my ass
My hopes of fortune are all gone
No A&R man wants to play my song
I just thought I'd learn to play guitar
I just thought I'd write another bar for you

My way of life don't understand
The power behind a company brand
Sister take a look at what you have
With your can of cola and your fag
I just thought I'd learn to play guitar
I just thought I'd write another bar for you

I hate that other businessman
Who  pushes drink and drugs on the young
And I hate that other businessman
Who wants to sell a war to sell a gun
I just thought I'd learn to play guitar
I just thought I'd write another bar for you

That's the way it is my fateful friend
I could never trust the Government
Because power is their God
They deal in everything including fraud
I just thought I'd learn to play guitar
I just thought I'd write another bar for you

And when I write my number one
I won't pretend I'm going to have some fun
And when my dream comes to be
I'm going to spill the beans you wait and see
I just thought I'd learn to play guitar
I just thought I'd write another bar for you

Dublin feels very small when the band breaks up, a backwater of pop up televisions shops and plastic seated cafés. Walking through the days on the same meandering route, canal paths and empty streets, just to do something; anything to leave the bed-sit for a while, contemplate the next move. Using the coffee money wisely, timing it so you'll meet a fellow muso, ever conscious of the time that's ticking.

## Jay Walking

You've got to leave you've got to grieve
You've got to get away
You've got to make it you've got to fake it
You don't have to stay

All of the people they're still waiting
For your stars to shine
Time is moving it is an engine
Going on down the line

Everybody's looking at you
Walking 'cross the street so vain
But I can guarantee you baby
They are waiting on you to fail

They didn't see what they did to thee
Building up your hopes
They let you down you hit the ground
But that was long ago

All of the people they're still waiting
For your stars to show
You act so reckless what were you taking
And does the Irish Times know

Everybody's looking at you
Walking 'cross the street so vain
But I can guarantee you baby
They are waiting on you to fail

It's going to stop this spinning top
You know that all things do
You've got to face it you've got to pace it
And that ain't nothing new

All of the people they're still waiting
For your stars to shine
You act so restless what were you taking
And is that baby mine

Everybody's looking at you
Walking 'cross the street so vain
But I can guarantee you baby
They are waiting on you to fail

Don't be cajoled don't sell your soul
You might be tempted kid
Keep it together don't trust the weather
You know I never did

All of the people they're still waiting
For what they already know
Time it moving it's like that jet plane
You can't say you didn't know

He didn't realise he was been used; was too soft, too open, needy for approval, came across as emotionally weak and foolish. An open book with no strategy for prudence and no appetite for confrontation: a real nice fellow. After internalising humiliations he found it easier to carry all the hurt and injustices than fight, put it down to his uniqueness, and so it began; the drift away from family and friends and eventually to the street. There you could hide your weak spot. After years alone he forgot what it was like to care and settled for a type of mysticism; a monk sitting on the busy pavement, tatty from the constant upheaval and drink.

## Mad Hatter

Nothing really matters to that old Mad Hatter
As he drinks all day in the sun
Even the two lovers are struck by how he suffers
It's the first time that they ever felt alone

As the storm clouds gather the lovers they grow
sadder
Looking for a doorway then they run
As the rain starts falling a mother takes her clothes in
While her two young children sing a song

But nothing really matters to that old Mad Hatter
As the rain seeps into his bones
The natural light is fading the neon lights are blazing
As the dirty city trundles on

In the bar rooms and the cafés everything is in place
But the other side of happiness is stoned
The volunteers are searching for the losers and
the urchins
As the night is turning very cold

But nothing really matters to that old Mad Hatter
He turns away he seen it all before
Yes nothing really matters to that old Mad Matter
As he waits for another day to dawn

I know because I was that boy
I know because I lived that life
I know because I did survive

Everything seemed so unusually quiet for the time of day. The only pubic house still hadn't opened, even the grocery store shut up shop and the local chipper too. Did he forget some national holiday or Catholic feast day, no, it was too eerie for that. Driveway gates were locked and tonnes of earth blocked the beach car park: on asking they said, 'the Knackers are coming'.

## Beggars and Vagrants

They didn't need you they didn't feed you
They didn't want you to stay
They didn't hug you they didn't love you
They just got in your way
They put their dirt loads on the approach roads
And you had to leave town
They didn't need you they didn't feed you
They didn't want you around

Your mother and children were yearning just to be free
While men and their fathers were looking on helplessly
Beggars and vagrants are scratching away at your walls
The laws they are made so you don't matter at all

They didn't nurture they had no culture
They didn't like how you sound
They felt above you they didn't love you
And they always look down
They always judged you they always shoved you
They set you up for to fall
They didn't embrace you they only chased you
and they put up a wall

Your mother and children were yearning just to be free
While men and their fathers were looking on helplessly
Beggars and vagrants are scratching away at your walls
The laws they are made so you don't matter at all

They stopped at nothing to make you go running
They even put up signs, 'That way'
They didn't charm you they tried to harm you
They tried to keep you away
They didn't want you to know what they knew
They tried to keep you outside
They tried to crush you they tried to rush you
Somehow you still survived

# Part Two

# Mammy's Boy

∞∞∞∞∞∞∞∞∞∞∞∞∞∞∞∞∞

Your Life and Tranquillity

Mother

Please Excuse Me

Blue Lights

Innocence Lost

The Marching Season

Futility of War Part 1

Homage to Sarajevo

Refugee

Gravitas

After the mass, a sixteen car cortège accompanied her to Glasnevin Cemetery, we lowered her down as the falling snow coated the coffin with a transparent veil of white.

## Your Life and Tranquillity

Mother in your eyes I saw compassion
In your face I saw gentleness
In your laughter I heard innocence
In your smile I saw hope
In your touch I felt kindness
In your words I heard honesty
In your arms I felt loved
In your dance I saw happiness
In your song I heard simplicity
In your dedication I saw strength
In your actions I saw humility
In your tears I saw my weakness
In your death I saw your life
Unburdened and at peace

'It's a sin to waste, God is good and keep the peace', was your philosophy. Devout innocence, intense with the Easter passion was your spiritual diet. The wisdom of clean living and a busy kitchen table instilled hope and righteousness.

## Mother

Mother loved you when she was strong
She was there for you when every little thing went wrong
Oh the summers her cooking smells
I was happy and she was looking oh so well
But there's one thing I forgot to tell
She carried her crosses like Jesus Christ she always fell
Like Jesus Christ she always fell

Time is moving like the rivers to the sea
There is nothing we can do but be free, but be free
Time is moving like the night upon the land
There is nothing we can do but understand,
but understand

Mother made you get along
Her life was simple but her love was oh so strong
'Up for work' her morning call
She was making sure that we would do no wrong
Snow was falling on the open clay
And I never, ever thought she'd go away
I always saw her here to stay

Time is moving like the rivers to the sea
There is nothing we can do but be free, but be free
Time is moving like the night upon the land
There is nothing we can do but understand,
but understand

'Dear Sir, Please excuse Martin for missing school yesterday as he had a cold'. The boy carried that same worded note to school many times. With his mammy gone now, the man had to write his own 'Please Excuse Me note' to the big bad world.

## Please Excuse Me

Please excuse me I'm an arrogant man
With a smirk on my face and power in my hand,
now you know
Please excuse me I'm a runner in
With a bent nose and a stupid grin, but I won't go
Please excuse me for causing you pain
I know it will never be the same again, ain't that so
Please excuse me for my big head
I know you're saying you wish I was dead
I don't think so

With my back to the wall I go
With my back to the wall I go
With my back to the wall,  my back to the wall
My back to the wall I go

Please excuse me for the way I talk
For the way I sing and the way I walk, it's so low
Please excuse me for being myself
You can always find yourself someone else, that you know
Please excuse me for being my own man
I know I don't fit into the plan, ain't that so
Please excuse me for the way
I live my life and get on with my day and all I know

With my back to the wall I go
With my back to the wall I go
With my back to the wall,  my back to the wall
My back to the wall I go

On a dark and lonely night in the back of a police car, a thing of beauty can have its genesis. They said that Blue Lights had the best intro to a song ever.

## Blue Lights

*'Okay Anto go on, Anto take a left,*
*go on take a left, break the lights,*
*they don't see ya, keep going, keep going, keep going*
*Turn left, turn left, turn left, we lost them now*
*We lost them*
*Put your foot down, put your foot down*
*Niall, are you okay in the back there, okay, okay lets go*
*Lets go, we're free now let's go*
*Colm open up the bottle, keep going, keep going,*
*We lost them now*
*Put your foot down'*

Well what do you know they came from behind
With their blue lights flashing and their sirens on
Yes those sirens were on
I tried to keep cool but my mouth got dry
I tried to act like a fool but I never could lie
No I never could lie

Did you ever get that feeling, nothing you can do
But you've got to be strong if you want to pull through
If you want to pull through
It seemed to last forever that back seat ride
I tried to keep it together but my tongue got tied
Yes my tongue got tied

Oh I wish I wish you were by my side
To protect me from the world outside
The world outside
It's a long long way from A to B
When you must pay with your liberty, your liberty
I can't believe it I nearly crossed that line
But I wasn't lucky to have an open mind
To have an open mind

It started becoming obvious that the Kool Kat Kid had a very neglectful home life, his mother didn't seem to care if he was hungry or not and left him to fend for himself while she put all her energies into her business empire. It came to a head when he was found half dressed, crying in the kitchen, staring into the empty fridge, after spending the night, home alone.

## Innocence Lost

I knew a boy could fill you with joy but I would cry
When I see the things that grown-ups can bring to magic eyes
I knew a boy could sing you a song and never shy
How can a love be left so unloved and I ask why

This is for every every every every every every every
Last good bye
This is for every every every every every every every
Victim's cry
This is for every every every every every every every
Innocent smile
This is for every every every every every every every
Wounded child

If God is alive he lives in a child but this can't be proved
Evil exits it is in the midst of those who rule
I knew a boy could sing you a song and never shy
How can a love be left so unloved and I ask why

This is for every every every every every every every
Last good bye
This is for every every every every every every every
Victim's cry
This is for every every every every every every every
Innocent smile
This is for every every every every every every every
Wounded child

They weren't even allowed to be Irish in their own country, that's what drove them to starve. You had so much sympathy for their injustice for their underdog status. The emotion rising with every black flag flowing, fudged the fact that violence begets violence. What could justify a mother's son lying lifeless and bloody on a border boreen; all his young summers gone, starkly stiff and soiled, yet happy memories still clean and innocent in her heart.

## The Marching Season

They pulled me up in Newry
Said they'd give it to me
Spit in my face and left me in a heap
In Portadown they judged me
A marching boy begrudged me
The debris of the riots lay on the street

In Coalisland I was careful
To act meek and cheerful
Being watched by an armed fascist with no receipt
In Limavaddy I got pissed
And a soldier with a lisp
Ordered me to kneel down and kiss his feet

In Belfast I heard some children
Saying they knew the difference
Their daddys' say the other side are cheats
On the border lay a body
With blood as red as any
And disgust ran from my head down to my feet

I thumbed a lift to Omagh
Put the balaclava on ya
A voice came softly from the other seat
By the time I got to Derry
There were seven comrades buried
Which side of the hateful fence I won't repeat

I met a mother in Strabane
Asked what side she's on
When she said the children's
I closed my eyes and wept

Having never been directly affected by war apart from feeling the shock waves of the Dublin bombings in nineteen seventy-four, he was still brutalized by the almost daily images and consequences of the low intensity civil war in the North. But the twisted burned out cars and hotels in Belfast and Derry were no preparation for the viciousness and horror in the news reels of places like Vietnam and Palestine.

## Futility of War Part 1

Close up and in rich leafy colour
Camera pans captured the terror, the panic
The confusion of young American rookies
Trapped in jungle clearances

Crawling towards the line of fire
The soundtrack of doom pinged with bullet whiz
Intermittent radio static
And strange voices of encroaching Vietnamese

Images displayed destroyed villages
Dazed dislocated faces staring blankly staring
While captured ill clad, ill nurtured young men
Were slapped, spit at, stripped and caned
And shot; unseemly in full view

Other unsteady footage
Bright in the white shimmering heat of the Levant
Replayed its own depravity
Forever etched in memory bereft of humanity

For over a year Sarajevo was under siege, the Serb forces held the high ground and enforced a blockade with a ruthless indiscriminate onslaught on the civilians below. But although the human family was ripping itself asunder, there was still an unquenchable human spirit trying to survive with acts of outrageous courage and profound dignity.

## Homage to Sarajevo

She had a brother she had a sister
She was playing out in the snow
Up came a soldier tied up and raped her
Down on her head came a crushing blow

She had a lover he had another
Long time since he seen her though
He was taken by the army
Who ethnic cleansed high and low

Look at the mountains look at the river
Look at all the red blood flow
Down on the streets of Sarajevo
Or anywhere the U.N. go

He had a gun he was only young
He couldn't go to school but still he know
How to use his index finger
Look at all those tracers glow

Living off rats and drinking urine
Underneath the no-fly zone
He had a dream he was in the sunshine
Looking at a T.V. show

Lord oh Lord oh lord, Lord oh Lord oh lord

While we persist with the quest for power and control there will always be refugees. Think Moses; think Wounded Knee and the Trail of Tears, think the Final Solution, the GULAG, Ballymun in the sixties. Think the Boat People, the Coffin Ships, think razor wire, walls and yellow stars.

## Refugee

God help you weary refugee
No matter what you've done
You're always going to face a soldier's gun

God help you weary refugee
No matter where you stand
You're always going to be in no-man's land

God help you weary refugee
And your sleeping child
God bless you going on your endless mile

God help you weary refugee
No matter what you're told
Night is falling and you're getting cold

God help you weary refugee
No matter where you are
You're always going to face a tougher law

God help you weary refugee
On your daily plight
You've got no home and now you've got no rights

God help you weary refugee
On this sun drenched day
They're going to make you move along the way

God help you weary refugee
No matter where you go
You're always going to face another foe

I know there's going to be a lot of dying
I know there's going to be a lot of crying

When the skyscrapers fell enveloping Manhattan in a thick grey toxic nebulas, it was like the world moved instantly into the new era of unconventional global war; a mist of fear descended that could not be contained. He thought of his deceased daddy and how much war he must have witnessed in his eighty five years.

## Gravitas

Everybody looked in horror and awe
Nobody believing what they saw
Smoke and flames and in two short hours
I was gazing at the rubble of the fallen towers

I have pity for all those who died
I have pity for all those who cried
I have pity for all those unfree
And the death of the dream of humanity

My daddy lived through the two world wars
Hiroshima and the Holocaust
My daddy saw his own country
Go up in the flames of bigotry

I have witnessed the Soviet fall
Star Wars and the Berlin Wall
I have witnessed Palestine
The dread and the sorrow of the human crimes

I have witnessed Bosnia
Kosovo, Africa and Chechnya
I have witnessed the horror of horrors
I'm looking in the face of the Holy war

I wanted to be with you on that fateful day
The very first time I heard the newscast say
I wanted to be with somebody I loved
I wanted to be there as soon as I could

Part Three

# The Street

∞∞∞∞∞∞∞∞∞∞∞∞∞∞∞

Dreamtime

The Dew

Fleadh

Tory

Ifika Youika

Rat World

Hypocrites Paradise

Dublin Pity

Baby With a Gun

Power Broker

You fell asleep to a summer symphony of birds; in the trees, hedge rows and out beyond the farmer's field on the estuary expanse. You awoke singing a song. In the funky state of half awareness made for the back room to guitar and tape recorder; the words, key and chords were exactly as you dreamt.

## Dreamtime

Real time can be dreamtime when you're going to stay
We could live this world in a perfect way
Look at all the love that's inside of me, and it's free

I'll see you there in dreamtime when you're passing through
Don't be afraid of dreamtime it is part of you
Look at all the love that's inside of me, and it's free

Real time it is dreamtime when you're here with me
It's something that is deep and nothing you can see
Look at all the love that's inside of me, and it's free

Stay with me in dreamtime there's no fast or slow
It is simply dreamtime there's nothing you should know
Look at all the love that's inside of me, and it's free

We will live like dreamers running out to play
Our souls as bright as silver nothing in our way
Look at all the love that's inside of me, and it's free

We'll always have that moon night; it's light defusing into the soft scented air of late summer grass, into furze flower essence mixed with the very mild perceptual tongue tang from waves that rise and fall against the rugged headland as it rests below the wash of the Milky Way. Our singularity event, oneness of flesh and soul, a beauty, a clarity, momentarily becoming one with the bending universal light; when the chaotic darkness is no more.

## The Dew

In the lane you said you loved me
As I blocked you from the wind
And your kiss was sweet and tender
And the stars began to spin
On that night we found our heaven
And our love was young and true
As I recall on the grass there was the dew

Then you asked me did I love you
I held you tight and said
Don't you know I'll always love you
'till the day they find me dead
And that night revealed its secrets
Never was a love more new
As I recall on the grass there was the dew

As I laid my coat beneath you
And our courting did begin
That night was filled with wonder
And the softness of your skin
Yes that night was filled with wonder
And we only had a few
As I recall on the grass there was the dew

The moon that shone above us
Reflected in your eyes
And the echo of the river
Matched the rhythm of your sighs
That night was really holy
The Gods blessed me and you
As I recall on the grass there was the dew

By night's end you were on the stream of joy with laughing eyes, playing in a circle of woodwind, rosin bow, goat skin, finger boards, vocal chords and varnished maple wood. In the afterglow of four days of musical stimulation you worked feverishly to get the essence of a first time Fleadh down in song.

## Fleadh

We drove into Listowel it was on the first Fleadh morning
We were very thirsty but we still put up the awning
The streets they were so full they were occupied by thousands
From every town in Ireland and from every single county

Cíarán brought his banjo and Murcheen brought his fiddle
Úna brought her singing songs and Rory brought his whistle
There were many people there and all types of banter
Looking for tradition to forget about the Planter

In the market square they were going through their paces
I dropped into a pub just to get myself acquainted
As the night progressed I was dancing at the céile
I even had a chance to meet my good friend Liam Ó Maonlaí

Next morning I was listy and I needed a concession
I dropped into a pub and I got into a session
The craic was mighty as they say in this part of Ireland
The pipers that were playing they were from the Scottish highlands

The weather it was fine and sure it was getting better
The bodhrán players they were playing jigs upon the leather
All the marching bands they took up positions
I was so enthralled just to see the good musicians

Then I had a chance just to give myself some pleasure
Seldom I indulge but I took an extra measure
When I turned around sure I saw the singing faces
I listened to the words and it was the Galway Races

A hundred thousand souls had Listowel a heavin'
On the third day of the Fleadh and it was the Sunday evening
My spirits they were high and I found it hard to say no
I looked up to the sky as I felt the great crescendo

The moon it cast it's spell on the whole proceedings
Everyone was dancing and it was a special feeling
People at the Fleadh all had good intentions
If you need a hand they will give you their attention

Are you going to the Fleadh sure you never will forget it
If you need a good excuse you never will regret it
I'll see you at the Fleadh for another rare occasion
Until then, slán go fóill agus sin é mise Éireann

The stay in Falcarraigh was like slowly opening the velum pages of a jewelled bound manuscript and taking part in the romantic tale: after jazz with Brent you crossed the open ocean to Tory to give the King his dues.

## Tory

We leave the pier of Magheroarty
Bound for a slice of land lying low
A dark thin line beyond the grave grey open ocean
The cheery talk of fellow farers keeps my mind at ease
Until it's time to raise my head
And see the green grey flank of Tory
Quay wall approaches fast to starboard
Dolphin breaks the sheltered waves
In an almost mocking saunter
Harmonious and Godlike
Its sleek black body rolls before us
Creating wonder then slips back under
While ropes are cast onto the land
And all onboard step onto Tory

I carry something under-arm for the King, Patsy Dan
A gift to be delivered
Sent by someone in Tír Chonaill
Now that distant other land
What type of garb will he have I wonder
That King that I must meet
Corduroy briefs and corduroy cap
Are on the man I finally greet
He has gold and silver but not too loud
And fine pens in his jacket pocket neat
But the sparks of brilliant colour
Come from his Gaelic speech
Those rhythms of an ancient world
Pushed further to the sea
Are spoken by two hundred souls
That call it home that treeless rock, Tory

As night falls sheaths of salty rain
Herald a storm with raging sea
While the King holds court in the only inn
Playing dancing songs on accordion
Rolled up sleeves and sturdy grin
Patsy Dan the Tory King invites me to join in and sing
The last hours of darkness
Are drunk away in the clubhouse shed
Where all the islands young descend
To resist the act of going to bed
They rave and splay on the sodden wood
As if possessed by the frenetic sounds
And psychedelic light display
Outside the unrelenting wind
Sends ghoulish howls across the narrow ruggedness
At daylight I will sail away
If the sea allows that to be
From this twilight land, Tory

On a beautiful summers morning you washed and dressed Napo for the last time. Then the hospice care nurse opened a small black medical case and filled a huge intravenous needle with a clear fluid, his eyes found yours; searching thoughts: are you ready!

Before Napo received the final dose the nurse asked what kind of music would relax him, you put on the Beatles. Napo relaxed as the Fab Four took him back to the hopeful promise and dreamtime of his heyday and died to the words 'life is very short and there's no time for fussing and fighting my friend'. You looked deep into his soul as his eyes dilated to black, the room filled with his essence in the warm luminosity of high summer.

Napo never knew the musical influence he had on you. And when you were very small he'd always sing the same tongue twister and dare you tenderly to repeat it: Ifika youika canika swimika lieika myika sonika Johnika I-itka willika givika youika a schillinika.

# Ifika Youika

If you, give-ika me-ika your-ika hand-ika I will
Give you, all the-ka love-ika I-ika can-ika give you
And if you give-ika me-ika your-ika smile-ika I will
Thrill you, all the-ka night-ika I-ika will-ika fill you

So shine your loving light on me
Shine your loving light on me
Shine your loving light on me

And if you, tell-ika me-ika that-ika you-ika want me
I will, give-ika you-ika all the-ka things you see
And if you, tell-ika me-ika that-ika you-ika need me
I will, do-ika all the-ka things-ika to be free

So shine your loving light on me
Shine your loving light on me
Shine your loving light on me

The rats turned the clay heap into a monster lair; they now only had to cross the fifteen feet of open space to access the abundance of waste food amongst the shrubs in the Afrikaners garden. The bigger rats held full slices aloft, inches off the ground and sped back only to return for more.

## Rat World

There's a rat in my back room
There's another in the hallway
There's one in the food store
Hope I don't find more

There's two in the ceiling
I can hear them squealing
There's one thing I fear
Hope I don't die here

I hope I don't die here
With those rats at my eyelids
Sucking on my eyeballs
Tugging at my torso

There's a rat-run in the kitchen
I hear them in the shower
And I leave the lights on
Every single hour

There are little baldy pink ones
Underneath the sink
I even saw a black one
Drinking from my milk

I hope I don't die here
With those rats at my eyelids
Sucking on my eyeballs
Tugging at my torso

They gnawed right through a brick wall
I guess their lair is too small
They're really getting cheeky
They're louder than the T.V.

They're resting on the futon
They're nesting in the bodhrán
One thing I fear
I hope I don't die here

I hope I don't die here
With those rats at my eyelids
Sucking on my eyeballs
Tugging at my torso

When we joined the EEC in the early seventies, serious amounts of monies in the form of grants came our way. Drifting closer to a corporate state; the cosy cartel of political power became over-confident, negligent of civic responsibility, greedy and ultimately corrupt.

## Hypocrites Paradise

You can change the ten commandments
You can change the laws to suit
You can break in little fragments
Anything you don't approve
You can have your own police force
You can have an army too
You can buy your own protection
To save you from the human zoo
When you have money

Yes it's getting easy, easy for to do
Yes it's getting easy, easier to fool you
When you have money

You can have a little island
A special place to rendezvous
You can meet the golden circle
The only work you'll have to do
You can have the biggest engine
Actually you can have two
You can gamble with the pensions
They will never get to you
When you have money

Yes it's getting easy, easy for to do
Yes it's getting easy, easier to fool you
When you have money

You can have the best attention
Tell the doctors what to do
There is no need for me to mention
You will never have to queue
You can mingle with the leaders
Meet the kings for scones and tea
You can kill and you can folly
You can act with impunity
When you have money

Yes it's getting easy, easy for to do
Yes it's getting easy, easier to fool you
When you have money

In the vacuum of semi-dilapidation the strong gravitational pull of hopelessness and peer pressure permeated the homes and streets of your youth. Vacuum packed heroin shipped in and cut, was the panacea; for the sole trader in death.

## Dublin Pity

Debbie seen the world like any other girl
Who's daddy wasn't there to lend a hand
She didn't see the point in going to school
She didn't see the point in doing exams

Debbie thought she had found true love
But the only thing she had was in her veins
Debbie took a drug and it wasn't love
She drifted through her life not far from dead

What I'm trying to say is not new baby
What I'm trying to say has been done before
What I'm trying to do seems a little crazy
And change your view of how you see the world

Derek grew up hard on these mean streets
Before he was a teen he could use a gun
Everyone around said someday
He would shoot his way into the underworld

Derek and his gang worked their way
From the corner store to the national vault
He couldn't read or write but he could plan
Every hoist down to its fault

What I'm trying to say is not new baby
What I'm trying to say has been done before
What I'm trying to do seems a little crazy
And change your view of how you see the world

Nothing's really changed since Debbie died
Crouched behind an alley wall
Everything she had was in her fist
It was the ring from Derek Hall

As her funeral passed the dirty streets
Another girl was looking for a fix
Everything estranged and it rained
But tonight she would pull some tricks

What I'm trying to say is not new baby
What I'm trying to say has been done before
What I'm trying to do seems a little crazy
And change your view of how you see the world

There are dirty needles and shitty lanes downtown.
There are street deals going down; hand to mouth, hand
to arse under the main street shop facades. There! Did
you smell that; the deodorant whiff of nihilism from the
successful gliding past, unfazed and unperturbed on their
highway to the stars.

## Baby With a Gun

I got a flat on the second floor
How was I to know what lay in store
The walls were so thin you hear them snore
When the lights went down you could feel them score

They're selling cocaine from number three
Anytime I pass they glare at me
There's a baby going wild above my head
Last night there was no sound so I thought it was dead

I went upstairs just for to see
I came to the door where I thought it should be
The door was open so I went right in
And I called out aloud 'is there anyone in'

There was blood on the walls
There was blood on the floor
There was blood in the hall
There was blood on the door

I saw something that no-one should see
Well maybe the State and its agencies
I saw something so depraved and vile
Like a Vietnam Vet my soul was soiled

I ran downstairs to my room below
And I looked out my window at the street below
Running down the alley where the junkies score
I saw the baby with a gun and a nappy sore

I asked myself where did it all go wrong
We have excess but we don't belong
I asked myself how did it get so far
We crave success but we don't know who we are

The hippies had a cautionary mantra about the perils of materialism, corporatism, environmental irresponsibility and human privation. The thought of all that free love, tree hugging and lentils would make any self respecting captain of industry stick his fingers down his throat to induce and produce vomit.

## Power Broker

Dead fish on the shoreline this world is getting old
The trees they are falling only to be sold
Hey Mister Power Broker it's all going wrong
The smoke that we're choking on is a human bomb

And I wish I was lying to you tonight
Yes I wish I was lying but I know I'm right

Depleted uranium falling onto the land
Distressed faces of children looking out from the sand
Hey Mister Power Broker it's all going wrong
The smoke that we're choking on is a human bom

And I wish I was lying to you tonight
Yes I wish I was lying but I know I'm right

It's a delicate balance the coral sea
It's a hell of a challenge just to be free
Hey Mister Power Broker it's all going wrong
The smoke that we're choking on is one of your bombs

And I wish I was lying to you tonight
Yes I wish I was lying but I know I'm right

## Part Four

---

# Place

The artist struggles all the time, like a masochist he won't give in to apathy. He's a fool we know, he won't let it go, that dream of a spiritual being; to speak his native tongue. Irresponsible to the extreme, he can't be swayed by failure, he knows best what it means to feel free and still dreams.

## Martin's Dream

When I was a younger man I had a dream
I could be a part of a mystical world
On the western seaboard speak a Celtic tongue
I could live and love with a deeper love
I would find the keys to my artistical world

Not much longer will I have to roam
This dream won't come much closer on its own
The soulful music I can hear
Oh the inspiration I know it's near

I can almost feel it my elusive dream
I can almost touch its golden seam
I can almost taste its nectar stream
I can almost tell you what she means

Pitching our tents beside a remote mountain lake, gazing into the stellar night looking for constellations, we found the Polar Star - It was our last time together as mountaineers.

## Mountain Man

It's another morning the sun is on the rise
Today I'm going to get myself together
Going to heed the warning of the changing skies
As the low clouds roll across the heather

And if it starts raining I won't feel deprived
It's the season for this type of weather
And if luck should leave me I won't need to sigh
The dices someday soon must fall together

Where mountain streams are flowing
Where all my dreams are growing

It's another evening the sun is going down
And the crimson light is all around me
There's another meaning to the words
'I'm coming down'
As I gaze onto the Sea of Tranquillity

And as that moon keeps rising the stars are all abound
I know the great bear points to the polar star
It's so easy believing that man was born free
When I realise where we are

Where mountain streams are flowing
Where all my dreams are growing

It's another morning the sun is on the rise
I find myself along the way
Looking at the beauty of every flower that's growing
Listening to what nature has to say

And if it starts raining I won't feel deprived
It's the season for this type of weather
And if luck should leave me I won't need to sigh
The dices someday soon must fall together

Where mountain streams are flowing
Where all my dreams are growing

Through a sheer act of will you forced your way into the Gaelic portal of song; a saga of fishermen: redemptive, celebrating the resilience of the human spirit and the Irish language community, that has survived tenuously for millennia on the western edge of Europe. 'Is trua do stór'- 'pity his love',

## Is Trua do Stór

Féach ar an fharraige, cad 'fheiceann tú
Seán Óg Ó Faoláin a chara amú
Istigh san fharraige, faoin gála glórmhar
Nach féidir cabhrú leis, is trua do stór
Is trua do stór, is trua do stór, is trua do stór

Ach cad a tharla bhí lá deas inniú ann
Bhí aimsir an-suaimhneach gan scamaill gan ghaoth
Cá bhfuil na bádoirí an bhfuil fhios againn
An bhfuil siad caillte, is trua do stór
Is trua do stór, is trua do stór, is trua do stór

Fan noiméad, fan tamaillín
Nach bhfeiceann tú fhéin tá an ghealach sa spéir
Fan noiméad, fan tamaillín
Nach bhfeiceann tú fhéin tá an ghealach sa spéir

Féach ar an fharraige, cad 'fheiceann tú
Seán Óg Ó Faoláin a chara ina shuí
Tá an bád san fharraige ag luascadh faoin seol
Éist leis an amhráin, na daoine 'seinnt ceol
Na daoine 'seinnt ceol, na daoine 'seinnt ceol, na daoine 'seinnt ceol

The ultimate and most profound acceptance of defeat is when the place names are changed forever, breaking the spiritual and historical connection. Ballybough means nothing; An Baile Bhocht means poor town. It was once the swampy marshy lands north of the River Liffey, outside the city walls close to the Tolka tidal estuary; home to brigands, refugees and the lowest caste. It was where Brian Boru was slain, where our brother lived and died.

## Ard Rí

Fuair sé bás ach níl sé imithe
m'Ard Rí, m'Ard Rí
Fuair sé bás ach tá sé beo fós i mo chroí
m'Ard Rí, m'Ard Rí
Fuair sé bás ach thug sé a lán grá dom nuair a bhí mé óg
m'Ard Rí, m'Ard Rí

'S as Baile Bhocht ó dhúchas mé
An áit álainn cois farraige
Ach tháinig na Gaill seo
Agus tháinig scrios
Ar an talamh agus ar ár dteanga

A lán droch scéalta dúnmháru agus gorta
A lán misneach orainn
Ach níl aon airm againn

Is cuimhin liom an lá
Nuair a tháinig siad ar a gcapaill ar an chladaigh
Bhí eagla an domhain orainn
Nuair a scaip siad amach ar fud na háite

Agus thit m'Ard Rí gan sciath ina phobal
Agus thug siad ainm nua ar mo bhaile

To get from the Pale to the Gael you must go west on the road, to the very west, to where you can see the red sun sinking into the Atlantic. There are a people there still, who have the tongue. You will see from the granite shore, Inis Meáin, Inis Oírr and Inis Móir and the limestone edifice of County Clare. You will feel happy there.

## Conamara

Ón Pháil go tír na nGael, bhuail mé siar an bhóthair
Agus d'fhan mé i mo shuí i gConamara
D'fhan mé i mo shuí i gConamara

Nuair a bhí mé óg d'éist mé leis an ceol
Agus shamhlaigh mé, mé fhéin i gConamara
Shamhlaigh mé, mé fhéin i gConamara

I mo thuairim fhéin níl aon áit chomh maith
Níl aon áit chomh deas le Chonamara

Feicim Inis Oírr, feicim Inis Meáin
Agus tá siad ina luí ó dheas ón nGaillimh
Tá siad ina luí ó dheas ón nGaillimh

Feicim Inis Móir, feicim Contae an Chláir
Agus cloisim na tonnta ar an trá
Cloisim na tonnta ar an trá

I mo thuairim fhéin níl aon áit chomh maith
Níl aon áit chomh deas le Chonamara

Before the ritual pot of tea was placed on the table, the King of the Hill always used to say in his jovial affable way 'Lig do scíth' let down your shield, let down your guard and relax.

## Lig do Scíth

Lig do scíth a stór mo chroí
Agus éist le mo scéalsa
An cuimhin leat fadó, fadó
Nuair a bhíomar le chéile

An cuimhin leat mo bhuachaillín
Nuair a bhíos an-sásta
Cad a tharla a stór mo chroí
Tá mé i m'aonar

Rinne mé rud dubhach
Agus d'fhág mé thú i mo dhiaidh
Níl fhios agam cá bhfuil tú fhéin
Ach tá fhios agam go bhfuil mé caillte

Lig do scíth a stór mo chroí
Caithfidh mé a rá tá brón orm
Ní fhaca mé ach an t-oileán úr
Ach ní fhaca mé do chroí bhriste

Lig do scíth a stór mo chroí
Agus éist le mo scéalsa
An cuimhin leat fadó, fadó
Nuair a bhíomar le chéile

Without your native tongue it was spiritual poverty, low self-esteem and dislocation. With it, it is alive, relevant, immediate and life affirming.

## Mar a Déarfá

Nach bhfuil sé deas bualadh le chéile
Nach bhfuil sé deas an ceol a chasadh
Nach bhfuil sé fíor, tá an aimsir ag athrú

Mar a déarfá, mar a déarfá, mar a déarfá
Mar a déarfá, mar a déarfá, mar a déarfá

Nach bhfuil sé deas mo theanga a thuiscint
Nach bhfuil sé an-dheas mo theanga a labhairt
Nach bhfuil sé fíor tá gach rud ag athrú

Mar a déarfá, mar a déarfá, mar a déarfá
Mar a déarfá, mar a déarfá, mar a déarfá

Nuair atá mé ag smaoineamh fútsa
Cuireann sé gliondar ar mo chroí
Tá an saol róghearr ná déan dearmad

Mar a déarfá, mar a déarfá, mar a déarfá
Mar a déarfá, mar a déarfá, mar a déarfá

An Irishman, Dublin to the core; city streets with their hungry knowledge learning him: be tough, survive, be smart and thrive. Kissing taller girls in twilight Fairveiw Park and choosing songs over smack, innocent craic. Imbued and shaped by the want to leave and need to stay and Miranda waiting at the quay.

## The Balladeer

I was born between the two canals
Fishmongers sang where Parnell stands
Not far away but far enough
We moved out of the tenement block
Just down the road to Ballybough
Not far away but far enough
The seagulls called in the early morn
As I walked to school through the traffic snarl
Not far away but far enough
As I grew the troubles blew
In Belfast and Derry too
Not far away but far enough
I fell in love we were so young
A broken heart she took my son
Not far away but far enough
Times have past and I've outgrown
All these things that I have shown
Not far away but far enough
So far away but not far enough

Part Five

# Consume

◇◇◇◇◇◇◇◇◇◇◇◇◇◇◇◇◇◇

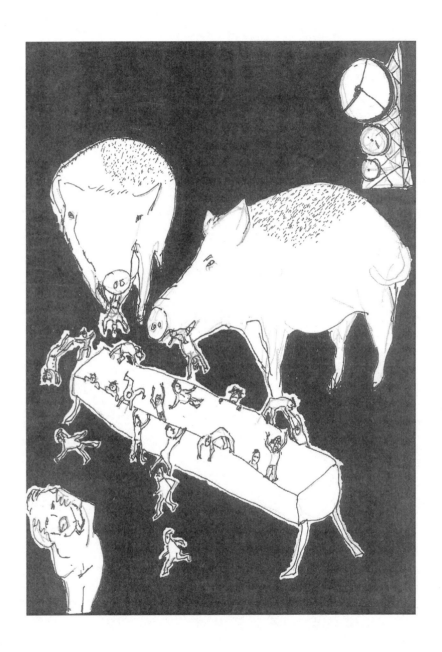

His thirty year descent was arrested by a rocky outcrop, inhaling deeply he took the chance to survey....the abyss. He chose not to choose a lifetime ago, abdication capitulation emasculation trepidation; frozen with fear, a social weed like the puny twig that protruded into the darkness beside him. Looking into that darkness he thought he saw a light sliver; it could have been a memory flash of the young man he used to be before the fall. Standing up, arms spread wide, Christ-like; he filled his lungs and flew.

## Begin Again

Leaves are falling winter's here once more
East wind calling the leaves are on my floor
Life has taken everything I had
Can you imagine anything more sad

When will we begin again, when will we begin
When will we begin again, again

Time is slipping like the melting snow
My friends I'm missing where did they all go
The moon keeps rising why does it not fall
As I was sleeping the son passed by my wall

When will we begin again, when will we begin
When will we begin again, again

Something's moving the sunset lets me know
It was not my choosing for to let you go
There are no choices there must be another dawn
There was rejoicing on the day that you were born

When will we begin again, when will we begin
When will we begin again, again

The visit in the world of dream was like a whale surfacing: for a fleeting moment the emotion was almost visceral. In that heightened openness you defined the haunted memories echoing, carving some beauty from the miscellaneous material of your life.

## Awoken

I awoke from a dream
And I thought I was still with you
I came from the streets
Where the lost and the lonely meet
I slipped back to my past
Just to see if it was all true
Was all true, was all true, was all true

I see your face with my eyes
And you know it was always you
It took me a life to realise
A life that time can't undo
A love as sweet as you
Will always find somebody new
Somebody new, somebody new, somebody new

I walked through the night
And the silence around me grew
I arrived at the dawn
Just in time for the changing view
I came to your door
Just to see that face once more
Your face once more, your face once more, your face once more

The thief of time, the thief of mistrust, the thief of conceit, the thief of forgetfulness all conspired - you became part of that conspiracy when you befriended the thief of delusion.

## Master Thief

Give me something I can hold on to
Give me something I can really feel
I won't fall for anything
If I don't think that it's real

I'm not one for miracles
I'm not one for blind belief
I need something for the passing time
Something for the Master Thief

Yes I understand this world
Empires rise and empires fall
Yes I understand this world
But would you come if I should call

Give me something from your deepest heart
Give me something you find hard to give
Give me something from your very soul
Something that you need to live

I'm not one for giving up
I'm not one for constant grief
Give me something for the passing time
Something for the Master Thief

Yes I understand this world
Empires rise and empires fall
Yes I understand this world
But would you come if I should call

When the phone call came that the King of the Hill died you were in the same farmyard kitchen where you both romanced and talked about the goings on in the world; where you washed down a million cups of tea and had easily a million laughs. You tried to take a leaf from his book and see death as part of life; thought you'd pull it off. But when you saw him in repose, a profound loss empty your heart; you lost a fellow jester and raconteur, a shepherd and planter of trees, you lost the most unlikeliest best friend, who always saw the good side.

## Nature's Room

Stars are out, moon is about, life in the vale
Seeds you've sown in the ground have not failed
When comes the spring birds always sing
Flowers always bloom in nature's room

Sun goes down, night comes 'round, mind how you go
Our hearts they need love we must sow
So go deep down nurture the ground
Keep you plough straight learn how to wait

Seems like our dreams are coming true
Seems like there's nothing we can't do
Seems like our loves come of age
Seems like there is one more page
Seems like the buds love the spring
Seems like I just want to sing

Standing on the kitchen table, the heat of incandescent light touching head, warm innocent laughter washing over you from the playground kitchen floor, waiting next in line to take your vitamin C: 'It's good for you and you have to take it' said Kitty, pretending to be stern. Squinting with the saccharine citrus tang you jumped into her arms, spinning, until you laughed with abandoned joy.

## Sister Love

In the morning we met the sun
We were conscious we were one
In the daytime beside the flowerbeds
We laughed forever in our heads

I won't forget that feeling
That we called love
I won't forget the meaning
Of Sister love

In the night-time beneath the filament light
We reached the corners of our life
In our dreamtime we travelled far
Always returning to where we are

I won't forget that feeling
That we called love
I won't forget the meaning
Of Sister love

Lying awake in the deadest hour just before the first bird braves the silence and heralds the new dawn, before the distant faint sounds of commerce from the waking city seeps into consciousness; in that complete space, a poem, whole and entire came. He knew from experience that if he didn't write it down straight away, the idea and emotional intent would slip, to be consumed into the oblivion of the stark day.

## Family Flame

How did it get so cold
It's like a little fire went out inside
Was it the frosty breath of others
That quenched the flames
Or did I forget to tend the ember sparks
As one by one they went too dark

Or was it every careless deed and cold disdain
That doused the delicate flames
With wintery rain
The hissing sound of every callous drop
Erasing every chance of light to stake its claim

So I've come knocking on your door
Looking for a match
The ones you sent before I never used
And now they're damp

If you have another one to spare
I'd strike it now and hold you close
And look as that tiny flame begins to grow
Just to know the glow of love is still there

The song waits to be finished, over a year it waits, three verses waiting to be resolved with hope, but nothing comes. It languishes on, will wait for years if necessary. Then out of a dream the boy returns and finds you in the flesh. You finish his song to sing to him.

## Before I Go

Before I go to the place below
Where nobody ever complains
Before I go and take my last throw
'cos nobody ever remains

Before I part into your heart
Where peace has been waiting so long
Before I move to the void unproved
I just want to sing you this song

I just want to tell you I loved you
You were never to blame
I just want to tell you I knew you
Before all of the pain

Now look the same stars are flickering
Above this road we're on
Behind us is darkness and loneliness
Before us is laughter and song

Before I pass and lie in the mass
And my soul is in a new plane
Before I cross and this chance is lost
There's something I want to explain

There was no countdown or preparation; the critical moment came shockingly and suddenly. In the pure violence of separation we bailed out simultaneously from opposite doors, free falling in the silence. The old war plane of our present, past and future surrendered to gravity, cart-wheeling slowly at first before breaking up until it disappeared in tiny fragments to the unknown. The only tangible thing to do in the aftermath was strum guitar and sing: that strange ability to process suffering quickly and express psychic wounds overtly, self-medicating to overcome despair.

## All This Way

You came all this way
Just to say how it would end
And you spent the day
Going through the years
I could not defend
I knew this day would come
But I didn't know how it would play
You were the only son
Now a strange man is in the way

The time has come to let you go
The time has come you let me know

When you asked me
How I survived without your love
I replied, it takes a certain kind to live that way
I might be still alive
But I died in every way
Then you arrived
For such a little while to make me pay

The time has come to let you go
The time has come you let me know

What I see is not the little child you used to be
You've changed with time
And lost the smile you had for me
I'm not surprised to see disdain in your eyes
I've so much to give
But you don't need a thing for me

The time has come to let you go
The time has come you let me know
The time has come to say good bye, good bye

It was getting darker, the light reflected red on the low tide sands of Sruwaddacon Bay below. We went back inside to the homely tuft fire heat of Big Joe's cottage, found succour in each other's company. A new word entered the camp lexicon that night; it described the new geo-technology of fracturing shale bedrock with a high pressure hydro-chemical solution to harvest methane gas and oil in the neighbouring counties of Leitrim and Fermanagh.

## Fracking Song

Did you hear about the story of Big Joe
Did you hear about the story of Big Joe
They came on his land gave him demands
Told him where the pipe was going to go

Did you hear about the ship called Solitaire
Did you hear about the ship called Solitaire
To Broadhaven Bay it came one day
Like a thief in the night it disappeared

I'm going down to Mayo before long
I'm going down to Mayo before long
That's where the gas is coming to ground
That's where injustice can be found

Everybody thinks we're wrong
But soon enough they're going to find
We're not going to be the ones
To steal their rights that were enshrined

Everybody thinks we're bums
Sees us as a running sore
But when the gas is all gone
They're going to come and frack for more

I'm going down to Rossport for a while
I'm going down to Rossport for a while
That's where my friends are holding the line
That's where they're spending their time

I'm taking the bus down to the camp
I'm taking the bus down to the camp
That's where you'll find equality
That's where I'm longing to be

I'm going down to Mayo before long
I'm going down to Mayo before long
That's where the gas is coming to ground
That's where injustice can be found

## 'NO TO UNFAIR WATER TAX'

The Troika didn't come to town for the shakedown, just made a quick call and our crew folded like a lovelorn school girl in the Sunday rain.

Supine and soft from their easy gain and hold of power and paralysed by fear of losing it all; they not only acquiesced but gave a pretext.

Like all shakedowns there was an implicit threat, and like all extortionists, small time gangsters or corporate: their moral laws have no empathy code. They will serve themselves and dominate: sociopaths.

## Water Tax Blues

This country is changing it's really changing
It's not the same country we used to know
When I look around me, when I look behind me
When I look above me, when I look below
All I can see are water tax meters under my feet

It's high time we stood up
It's high time they knew
It's high time we told them
What the poor can do, can do, can do

To all the people change is coming
But that is something you already know
To all my people what you must do
Is to be ready don't let them know
All I can see are water tax meters under my feet

It's high time we stood up
It's high time they knew
It's high time we told them
What the poor can do, can do, can do

Throughout our history, penal laws and penury
The Great Hunger not long ago
It's not my place to try to incite you
But that's where we came from now where will we go
When all I can see are water tax meters under my feet

It's high time we stood up
It's high time they knew
It's high time we told them
What the poor can do, can do, can do

Such a noble thing, Erin go Bragh, emblazoned in gold with the harp and shamrock, such a noble symbol of nationhood, music and the green earth, such fragility in the face of venality. That's the trouble with all the poor poets dreams, they are no match for the march of the conglomerates, the magnates, the new landed class, salivating on the first taste of financial power: We can keep the name its good for business.

## Erin go Bragh

Did you hear the story of Billy McGuire
He had some pigs that he robbed from the Squire
And although these pigs were scrawny and small
He fed them with meat that he robbed from the stall

Within a year these pigs grew so strong
All were amazed how those pigs came along
And Billy McGuire saw his power rising fast
But he needed more meat 'cos the pigs wouldn't fast

In the refugee camp there was many a child
With faces so lost and eyes that were wild
Billy McGuire got an idea at last
He would make all those children useful at last

He knew the General who managed the camp
And offered him shares in his pigs for a chance
To unburden his hands from the waifs and the strays
And the prospect of wealth for the end of his days

In the beginning it started with one
A young girl called Suzy with hair long and blonde
A pig they called Mathew crunched on her skull
And the munching continued 'till she was all gone

The pigs grew so big now they needed much more
So Billy McGuire paid for the road

To transport his cargo without stop or delay
He hired all the soldiers to make clear the way

The pigs always had their snouts in the trough
And the screams of the children were never far off
But more land was needed to quench the pig's greed
So the Council was bribed to change all the deeds

Billy McGuire took a seat on the Board
The press they all said he was a man of his word
A famine was brewing the people subdued
But the pigs they dined on the freshest of food

The hands of the clock are ticking so fast
The price of the pigs have increased with their mass
Now Billy McGuire is a billionaire
And he's looking for markets to increase his shares

Alone in his office there's a map on the wall
The smile on his face can be seen from the hall
'I'll buy that island that looks like a pig
On its own in the ocean called Erin go Bragh'

## Post Script

Do Shorcha

********

Mile Buíochas Le

Lorcán

&

Donncha

&

John Seáinín